ALEXANDER GRAHAM BELL

Andrew Dunn

The Bookwright Press
New York • 1991

Pioneers of Science

Alexander Graham Bell
Archimedes
Karl Benz
Marie Curie
Michael Faraday
Guglielmo Marconi
Isaac Newton
Leonardo da Vinci

First published in the
United States in 1991 by
The Bookwright Press
387 Park Avenue South
New York, NY 10016

First published in 1990 by
Wayland (Publishers) Limited
61 Western Road, Hove
East Sussex BN3 1JD, England

© 1990 Wayland (Publishers) Limited

Library of Congress Cataloging–in–Publication Data
Dunn, Andrew.
    Alexander Graham Bell / by Andrew Dunn.
      p. cm. — (Pioneers of science)
    Includes bibliographical references and index.
    Summary: Examines the life and accomplishments of the speech
teacher whose study of sound and the human voice led to his invention
of the telephone.
    ISBN 0–531–18418–8
    1. Bell, Alexander Graham, 1847–1922—Juvenile literature.
2. Inventors—United States—Biography—Juvenile literature. [1. Bell,
Alexander Graham, 1847–1922. 2. Inventors.] I. Title. II. Series.
TK6143.B4D86 1991
621.385'092—dc20
[B]
[92]   90–2628
                                            CIP
                                          AC

Typeset by R. Gibbs & N. Taylor, Wayland
Printed in Italy by Rotolito Lombarda S.p.A.

Contents

1 ▽ Introduction

When Alexander Graham Bell was a young boy in Edinburgh, Scotland, the Victorian era was reaching the peak of its activity. It was an age of great discovery, invention and exploration, of expanding British empire and industry. Huge factories and cotton mills, powered by coal and steam, belched smoke from their chimneys. There was no electric light. Main city streets were lit by gas lamps, as were some houses, though many people used lamps burning whale oil or paraffin. Bicycles were an exciting new form of recreation and transportation. Railroads were spreading at home and abroad, and iron steamships were replacing wooden sailing boats. The electric telegraph had just arrived in Edinburgh, which meant that for the first time signals could be sent from London in seconds.

During Bell's early life, factories and ironworks were becoming common sights in Europe and North America.

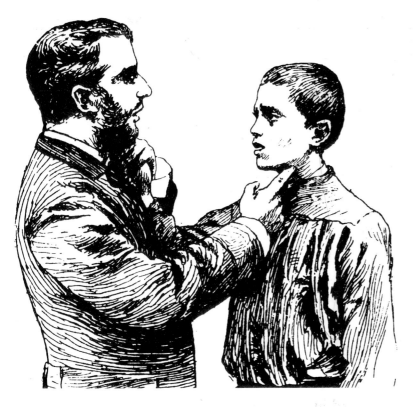

Bell helped many deaf children to speak. One way they could learn was by feeling the teacher's throat as he spoke, then trying to make their own throats vibrate in the same way.

There was no radio or television. People entertained each other with conversation, reading, or singing around the piano. Lectures in public halls were very popular with the new middle classes, eager to improve their education. Such people were anxious to learn to speak well, and elocution lessons were common. Speech, language and the voice formed a respected branch of science. Bell's father was a "Professor of Elocution and the Art of Speech," which sounds strange today; now he might be called a speech therapist. Alexander, too, became an expert on speech.

We would hardly recognize the world in which Alexander grew up. In our world of satellites, video links and computers, it is difficult to imagine life without the telephone. But it took the brilliant imagination and determination of Alexander Graham Bell to think of it, and to struggle against the odds to make it work.

To understand how Bell turned the telegraph into the telephone, it helps to understand a little about electricity and magnetism. The two cannot be separated. An electric current flowing through a wire always produces a magnetic field around it. Similarly, a magnet moving near a wire induces, or sets up, an electric current in the wire.

The flow of an electric current depends on the electrical resistance of the wire. Copper is a good conductor of electricity, because it puts up very little resistance. If the resistance changes, then so does the flow of current. It is like making a water pipe wider or narrower.

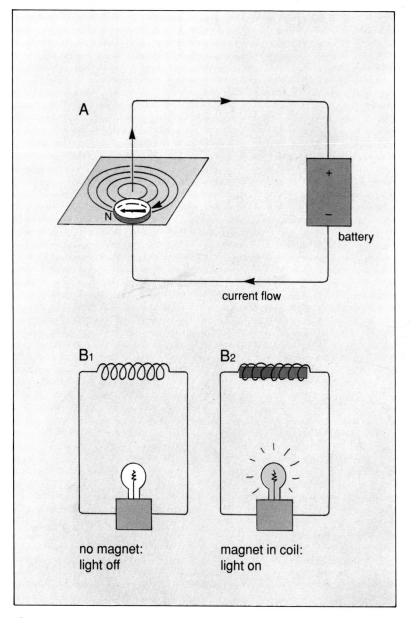

A

battery

current flow

B₁

no magnet:
light off

B₂

magnet in coil:
light on

In diagram A, a current of electricity flowing along a wire sets up a circular magnetic field around the wire. The stronger the current, the greater the magnetic force becomes. In B1, the magnet is not in the coil so there is no current. In B2, the magnet in the coil causes the current to flow around the wire.

A deaf child watches her teacher, trying to copy the sounds. By watching herself in the mirror, she can see whether she is using her lips and tongue correctly.

Sound is carried through air by the vibrations of the air particles, each bumping into the next, sending the sound waves outward like ripples on a pond. If those vibrations could somehow be imprinted on an electric current, wires could carry sound much farther than air could. But even though these facts about electricity and magnetism were known before Bell was born, people said carrying speech on wires was ridiculous – and impossible. But Bell, who knew very little about electricity, proved them all wrong.

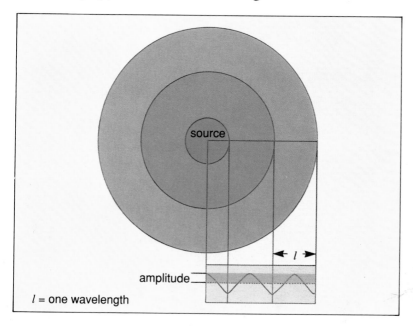

source

l

amplitude

l = one wavelength

A diagram to show how sound waves spread out from the source like ripples on a pond. The distance between each ripple is the wavelength. The amplitude is a measure of the loudness of the sound.

7

Alexander Graham Bell was born in Edinburgh in March 1847, in a small apartment in the city's elegant Georgian "New Town." The second of three brothers, he was christened simply Alexander Bell, but his family always called him Aleck.

His father, Alexander Melville Bell, studied and taught speech at Edinburgh University, cured defects such as stammering and wrote popular books on elocution. Aleck and his brothers, Melville, "Melly," and Edward, "Ted," did not go to school at first; their mother, Eliza, taught them at home, although she was very deaf. Aleck was interested in everything. He was very musical and an excellent pianist. He also loved anything to do with the theater.

With the famous castle dominating the skyline, and the spire of Scott's monument overlooking Princes Street, the Edinburgh of Bell's youth looks little different today.

Bell's father thought that spending time in the Scottish countryside would improve Aleck's health.

When Aleck was eleven, a family friend named Alexander Graham came to visit. Aleck liked the name so much he decided to adopt it, to show his independence. From then on, he called himself Alexander Graham Bell.

Aleck's father felt that living in the smoky city was bad for his children, so he bought a second house in the country. It made a wonderful playground for the boys, and the countryside fascinated Aleck. He studied birds, plants and flowers and would often take dead animals back to the city house to dissect them there with the help of his friends.

In 1858, Aleck was sent to the Royal Edinburgh High School. He hated the formal lessons of Latin and Greek and he was never a distinguished pupil. When he left school, aged fifteen, his grandfather was alarmed at his grandson's lack of academic progress and called him to his London home. During the following year, Grandpa Bell, who was also a speech expert, taught Aleck his special skills. Aleck obediently learned many speeches from Shakespeare's plays by heart. He discovered that serious study could be both challenging and exciting. He became a studious, thoughtful young man.

9

Edinburgh University in the 19th century. Aleck's father taught there, and Aleck himself studied Greek and Latin at the university.

When Aleck went home to Edinburgh, his father challenged him and his older brother Melly to make a mechanical voice, based on one Aleck had seen in London. They used wood, string, rubber, a tin tube for the throat, and their own lungs. When Melly blew into the tube and Aleck worked the flexible tongue and lips, the machine made a harsh "quacking" sound – like the voice we associate with Donald Duck. Their triumph came when they made it say "mama" so convincingly that a neighbor came to see what was wrong with the "baby"! The experiment taught Aleck how the human voice worked in great detail.

In Edinburgh, Aleck missed the independence he had had in London. At home his parents supervised everything. He felt restless, and even made plans to run away to sea. But at the last moment, he changed his mind. He had already decided to be a teacher. So he applied secretly for a job at a school in Elgin in northern Scotland. He did not mention his age (sixteen) and even gave as a reference a certain Professor Alexander Melville Bell of Edinburgh – his own father! His father soon found out, but he was a sensible man and allowed Aleck to go. For a year, Aleck taught music and elocution as a student teacher. Fortunately he looked older than he really was, for he was younger than some of his pupils.

Aleck then spent a year learning Greek and Latin at Edinburgh University before returning to Elgin. During the long, dark, winter evenings, Aleck spent hours in his room experimenting with his voice, tapping his throat and cheeks with his fingers while making different vowel sounds, and whispering at tuning forks of different pitches. He was trying to find the precise pitches at which the mouth resonated when making different vowel sounds.

When the prongs of a tuning fork are struck, they vibrate at an exact frequency, depending on their length. This one vibrates 440 times per second, producing the note that musicians call "A."

11

Later he discovered that a German scientist, Hermann von Helmholtz, had already done the same experiments. Von Helmholtz had used tuning forks, kept vibrating by electromagnets, to create artificial vowel sounds. Aleck did not quite understand it and became mistakenly convinced that von Helmholtz had managed to *send* his vowel sounds by electricity, rather than just making them. Aleck's throat-tapping experiments were his first step along the road to the invention of the telephone.

Aleck spent the next year teaching in Bath. He decided he must learn about electricity, so he bought some chemicals and bottles to make batteries with, and strung wires from his bedroom window into a friend's window two houses away. Slowly he began to learn a little about electricity and the telegraph.

Meanwhile, Aleck's parents had moved to London, where his father had scored a great success. For many years, speech scientists had been trying to invent a special alphabet in which the signs would stand not for letters but for actual sounds, so that any noise in any language could be written down and read by someone else. Such an alphabet would help the study of language enormously. After fifteen years, Aleck's father finally produced an alphabet, which he called "Visible Speech."

As thousands left Britain to seek a better life in North America, scenes like this at Portsmouth Dock were common. In 1870, Aleck and his family set sail for Canada.

Joining his parents after the school year ended, Aleck began working late, often until long past midnight, and sleeping late, a habit he kept all his life. He continued his experiments on the voice. He had a pet dog, a stray Skye terrier. By manipulating its jaw and throat, he persuaded it to make the sounds, "ow ah oo ga ma ma," which, to Aleck's imaginative ears at least, sounded remarkably like, "How are you, Grandmama?"

He also began to teach two deaf children how to talk, using his father's system. After a few lessons, the children could say many words.

Then tragedy struck the Bell family. Both Aleck's brothers had suffered from ill health, and Ted had died in 1867, at the age of only seventeen. Now, in 1870, Melly, too, fell ill and died. Aleck and his parents were heartbroken. Aleck's own health had been worrying his parents for some time. Remembering how a trip to Canada when Melville (Aleck's father) was young had saved his health, they persuaded their only remaining son to come with them to start a new life in North America. On July 21, 1870, Aleck and his parents set sail across the Atlantic for Quebec, Canada.

Today, deaf children can learn by using modern electronics and by playing musical instruments. However, many of Bell's principles for teaching the deaf remain the same.

In August 1870, the Bells landed at Quebec. Within a week they had bought a house at Tutelo Heights in Ontario, above a town called Brantford, not far from the Niagara Falls. Aleck spent the rest of the summer reading and lying among the trees. By the autumn, his health was completely restored.

Meanwhile his father was visiting different cities, giving lectures on Visible Speech. In Boston, an American city famous for its science and education, he met Sarah Fuller, who had just started a school for deaf children. She asked Melville to teach her Visible Speech so that she could use it there. Melville was too busy, but Aleck was eager to try.

14

So the nex... ...on. At Miss
Fuller's Sch... ...teaching the
deaf boys a... ...d taught deaf
children i... ...isible Speech
and draw... ...e mouth and
tongue... ...lts were very
encoura...

Back... ...Aleck thought of
those c... ...and lost they must
feel; a... ...rom the real world
just h... ...e decided he would
devo...

I... ...is own school in his
re... ...a dozen deaf pupils.
In... ...into the night, he took
o... ...nets, and experimented
... ...ing the telegraph.

... knowledge of music and
... ed side by side, and a note
... ote can be heard from the
... string in the first piano
... d, or frequency, depending
... high note; slowly for a low

The frequency of sound waves is measured in cycles per second, or Hertz (Hz). Humans can hear sounds from about 20 Hz to 20,000 Hz.

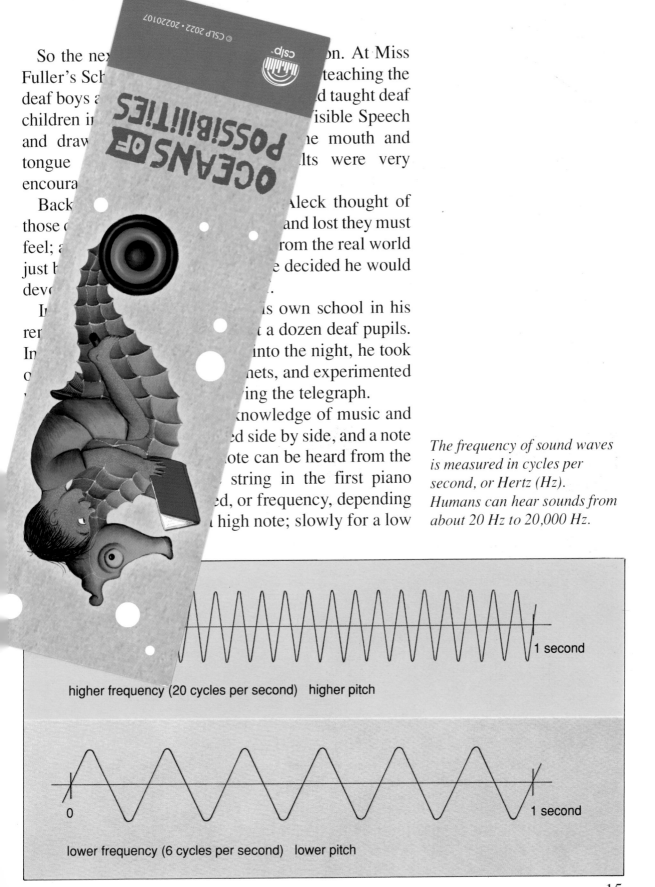

1 second

higher frequency (20 cycles per second)   higher pitch

0

1 second

lower frequency (6 cycles per second)   lower pitch

15

The telegraph

At that time the only way of communicating quickly over long distances was by telegraph. A person wanting to send a message would take it to a telegraph office, where an operator would translate it into the dots and dashes of Morse code, which he tapped out on a special key like a switch. When the key was pressed, briefly for a dot, slightly longer for a dash, a current from batteries was sent down a wire to another office, which could be in another city. There, another operator listened to the dots and dashes and translated the message back into words. Because of the way it worked, each wire could carry only one message at a time. Bell began to work on a way of sending several at once.

This early Morse telegraph transmitter was made in 1835.

note. The sound is carried by the air vibrating. Of all the strings in the second piano, only one naturally vibrates at the same frequency – the one for the same note. It picks up the vibrations from the air and it too starts vibrating.

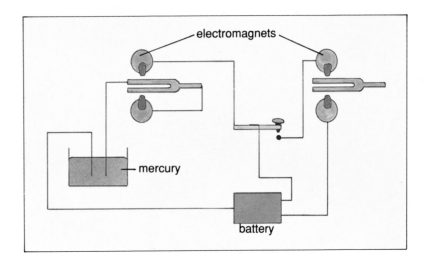

Bell spent months making a rapid switch using a tuning fork with a wire dipping into liquid mercury. The forks at each end were placed between electromagnets.

Bell thought that he could apply that idea to the telegraph by using vibrating electricity instead of air. He used a tuning fork vibrating at a precise frequency to make an electric current switch on and off at the same rate. The current switched an electromagnet on and off at the other end of an electric circuit. He thought the vibrating force of the magnet would set a tuning fork of exactly the same pitch vibrating, but would have no effect on any other tuning forks. Then he could use several tuning forks, each of which would sound only its partner in a matching set at the far end and not the others. That way each pair could send and receive its own messages without interfering with others being sent on the same wire.

It was a simple idea, but it took Bell a whole year to make it work at all. His equipment needed very careful adjustment, and Bell was not very good with his hands. His moods swung between wild enthusiasm and gloomy despondency. He was afraid that someone might copy his idea, so he kept everything locked during the day. After a year of teaching by day and experimenting by night, he was worn out. He spent the summer of 1873 resting with his parents in Canada.

That autumn Bell returned to Boston to take a new job – as Professor of Vocal Physiology at the new Boston University. He moved too, to stay with a wealthy man named Thomas Sanders and his wife.

Another of Bell's early inventions was the phonautograph (sound-writer). Speech made the stylus scratch a wavy line on the smoked glass below. Bell hoped that deaf pupils could learn by copying patterns made by hearing speakers.

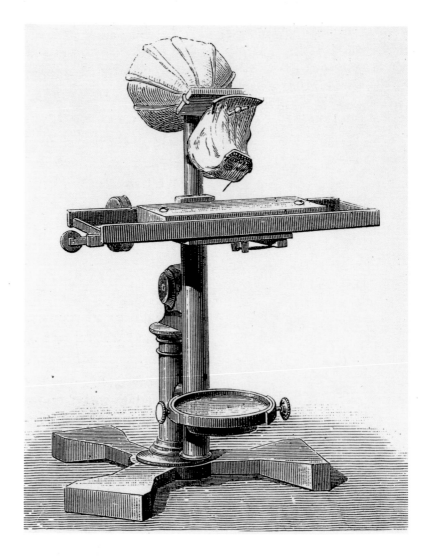

Their son Georgie was six and had been born deaf. Bell had already been teaching him for a year, and now he taught him to read and spell.

Bell was still experimenting with his multiple telegraph idea. For his experiments he often needed new pieces of apparatus, which he used to have made at "Williams" electrical shop in Boston. The dingy cluttered shop and its workshops were favorite haunts of local inventors. Some of them were cranks, but others, like Thomas Edison, who invented the phonograph and the electric light bulb, had real genius. One of the assistants at "Williams" was a clever young man named Thomas Watson. Watson found himself helping Bell more and more.

All Bell's experiments had to be done in his spare time. His real work was teaching his deaf pupils and his university students, and spreading the message about Visible Speech. Yet his thoughts were mostly of the multiple telegraph. If he could make one that really worked, it would be worth a fortune. A telegraph company could send many messages at a time and make much more profit. But Bell was hampered by his lack of electrical knowledge. As each new problem cropped up, he struggled to find a way around it, only to find another problem.

A new idea

During the crowded year of 1873, Bell had a flash of genius, although he did not see its importance until later. Instead of using a vibrating tuning fork to switch a current on and off very quickly, he realized that if he used a vibrating strip of thin magnetized metal near a coil of wire, it would set up in the coil a continuous current. This current would change in strength as the strip moved up and down. Batteries would not be needed. However, he thought the current would be too small to be of any use, so he did not even test this idea. But there at the back of his mind, waiting to be put together, were all the ingredients he needed to produce the telephone.

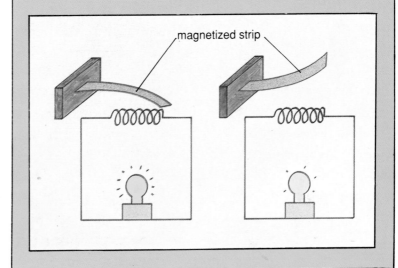

A diagram to show the principle behind Bell's moving strip experiment.

4 The Telephone Is Born

One day in July 1874, at his parents' house near Brantford, Bell suddenly knew it must be possible to transmit speech by electricity. In his resting place under the trees, he sketched a very basic "harp" telephone, so called because it would consist of many differently tuned metal strips, like the strings on a harp. Each strip would respond to a different pitch of vibration in the air, and together they would transmit the whole range of pitches that make up speech. He did not have the skill to make the harp, and he did not think it would transmit very far. Besides, the multiple telegraph seemed more important. So the harp telephone remained just a sketch.

The next winter he worked harder than ever on the multiple telegraph by night, while he taught by day. One of his deaf pupils was a fifteen-year-old girl named Mabel Hubbard, daughter of Gardiner Hubbard, one of the wealthiest businessmen in Boston. Scarlet fever had left her completely deaf from the age of five. Her father had become a strong campaigner for helping the deaf to learn to speak.

Bell mentioned his work to Gardiner Hubbard over tea one day, not knowing that Hubbard was in a better position to help him than anyone else in Boston. Hubbard had been fascinated by telegraphy for years and was convinced that the giant Western Union Telegraph Company was making too much profit. Hubbard and Thomas Sanders offered to help him patent his inventions, in return for equal shares of any profits. If Bell's inventions proved valuable, they would form a company to take advantage of them, each with equal shares. It was the beginning of what later became one of the biggest companies in the world.

They all knew that there were other inventors

working on similar improvements to the telegraph. Bell worked furiously, sometimes till dawn, solving problems and making improvements. At the end of February 1875, he patented a device called an "autograph telegraph" (writing telegraph). It used the multiple telegraph ideas to make several simultaneous lines of dots and dashes on a strip of paper. It was a primitive version of the modern facsimile (fax) machine.

A few days later, Bell was in Washington, D.C., the capital of the United States. He called on Joseph Henry, the most famous American scientist of the time, who had invented the first electromagnetic telegraph. Bell mentioned his harp telephone, and a more recent idea of using a diaphragm (membrane) instead of many separately tuned metal strips. Henry thought the basic principle would work. "It is the germ of a great invention," said the old man. When Bell said he doubted he had enough electrical knowledge to perfect it, Henry's reply was simply: "Get it!"

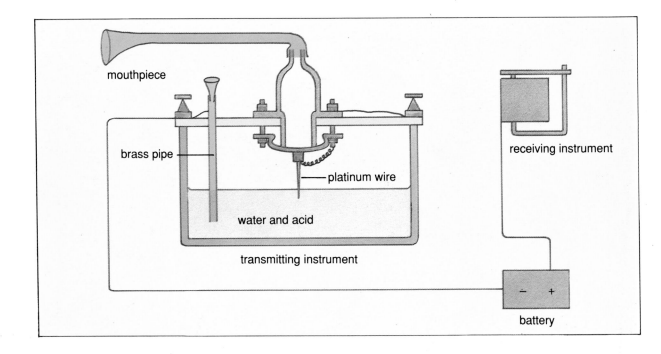

mouthpiece

brass pipe

platinum wire

water and acid

transmitting instrument

receiving instrument

battery

− +

A diagram of Bell's diaphragm telephone, adapted from one of his notebooks.

Bell returned from Washington exhausted. He gave up his private pupils, except for little Georgie Sanders, so that he could concentrate on telegraphy. Now his only income was from the university and he was very short of money.

Hubbard thought the autograph telegraph would make the most money, so he wanted Bell to concentrate on that, but Bell found it very difficult to make the device work. He persevered, but his mind was full of his dream: to transmit speech.

He still thought a vibrating magnetic strip would produce a current too small to be of any use, although he still did not test whether that was true. Instead, he thought of a way around the "problem": variable resistance. The current passing through a wire grows as the wire's resistance weakens. If he could find a way of making the resistance in a circuit vary according to the vibrations of sound, then he could pass a current as strong as he liked along the wire, and as the vibrations changed the resistance, the current would change, carrying the pattern of vibration with it. He experimented with the idea briefly, but without success, and went back to the autograph telegraph.

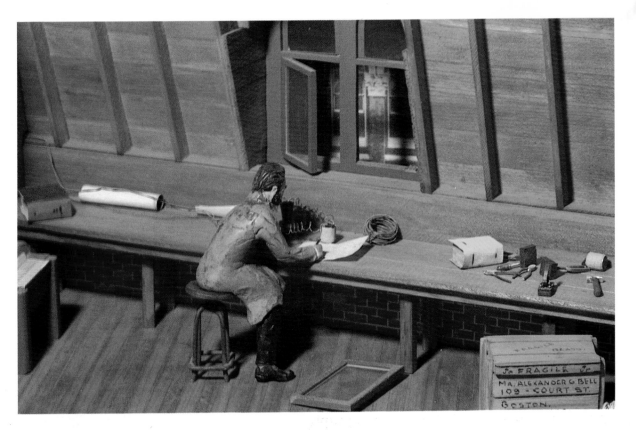

June 2, 1875, was a hot day in Boston, and hotter in the attic over "Williams" shop. Bell and Watson were making more changes to the multiple telegraph part of the instrument. They were in different rooms, each with three transmitters and three receivers, all joined by one wire between the rooms. As often happened, one of the metal strips on Watson's receiver jammed stuck. Bell, who hated hot weather, crossly turned off the transmitters and the batteries, and shouted through to Watson to twang the strip free. As Watson did so, Bell happened to be watching the matching receiver in his own room. To his astonishment, it vibrated all by itself. Bell darted through to Watson, told him to keep plucking, and dashed back. Still the other receiver responded. Quickly, Bell disconnected everything except the receivers. The sound grew stronger. Bell knew what it meant. His idea of the previous year, which he had never tried, worked. The strip did produce a strong enough current, all by itself, to make its matching receiver respond. The telephone was born.

The attic room in which Bell invented the telephone has been re-created in the Bell Museum, Boston. This model shows Bell at work in March 1876.

5 The Telephone Grows Up

After a few more experiments that evening, Bell stopped to think. A diaphragm would surely be better than a lot of metal strips. He sketched an instrument using a diaphragm and asked Watson to make two of them. Watson quickly made one of the instruments, but the diaphragm he used was too thin and broke when they tested it. They tried a stronger membrane, but even

The telephone works

Bell had still not made a telephone that actually transmitted speech, but he knew he could. He rented some rooms of his own, and on March 8, he started his telephone experiments again with Watson. On the afternoon of Friday March 10, 1876, Bell was in one room with a transmitter and Watson was in another with his ear pressed to a receiver. Just then Bell spilled some acid on his trousers and, without thinking, shouted into his mouthpiece, "Mr. Watson, come here, I want you." To his astonishment, Watson came. The telephone worked.

Opposite This may look nothing like a telephone, but it is the first of Bell's instruments to transmit speech. In fact, a modern mouthpiece is quite similar, but much smaller.

though it transmitted the sound of a voice, no words could be made out. Then Watson fell ill and nothing more was done with the telephone for months. Bell's mind was on other things.

He had been teaching Mabel Hubbard since she was fifteen. Now she was seventeen, and he was just twenty-eight. He realized he loved her. On Mabel's eighteenth birthday, November 25, 1875, they became engaged.

Bell was still not free to work on the telephone. He had his teaching, and he had to write a foolproof patent application for his telephone, before anyone else stumbled upon the idea. Above all Bell needed money, and while he was earning, he was not inventing.

Bell finished writing his patent in January 1876, but he did not send it to the patent office right away. Because he was British, he wanted to patent the telephone in Britain first. It turned out later that the man who had taken the application to England never dared take it out of his suitcase. He thought people would laugh. Many people in the United States laughed at Bell's idea, until they heard it working.

Eventually Gardiner Hubbard lost patience and officially handed the patent in to the U.S. Patents Office on the morning of February 14, 1876. He was only just in time. That afternoon, another inventor named Elisha Gray handed in a document saying he claimed as his invention "the art of transmitting conversations through an electric circuit." But Gray had not actually tried out his idea. So Bell was granted the patent as inventor of the telephone: U.S. patent number 174,465. It was to become one of the most valuable patents ever issued.

Elisha Gray invented a telephone, but when Bell patented his own telephone, Elisha Gray's instrument was only a sketch.

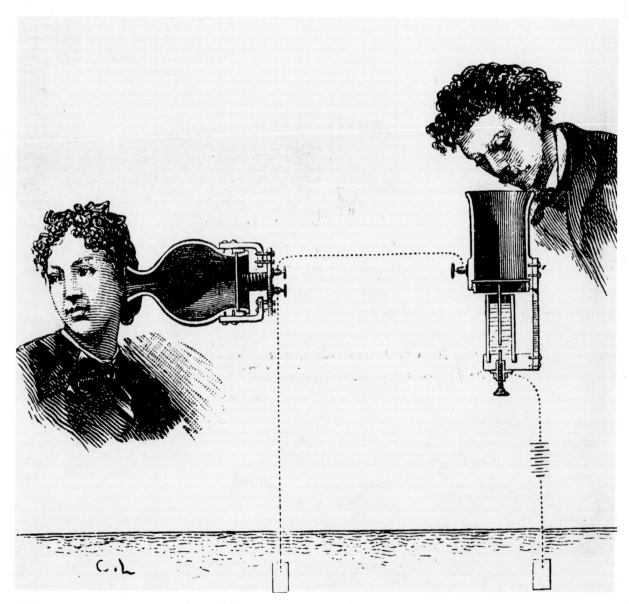

1876 was the hundredth anniversary of the United States' Declaration of Independence. Among the many celebrations was the huge Centenary Exhibition in Philadelphia. There were exhibits from all over the world, of art, industry and science. Elisha Gray was exhibiting his telegraphic inventions, and Bell felt he could not compete. But in June, he was persuaded to show some of his inventions, and his telephone took its place in a quiet corner among the electrical exhibits.

The exhibits were judged by notable scientists, and the Emperor of Brazil, who had opened the exhibition. At the last minute they came to look at Bell's equipment. Bell spoke to them from across the exhibition hall. The Emperor took the receiver and listened. Suddenly he jumped out of his chair and cried, "I hear! I hear! It talks!" The telephone became the star of the exhibition.

The great Centenary Exhibition of 1876 drew thousands of visitors to Philadelphia. Bell's telephone became the prize exhibit.

SALEM

THE TELEPHONE

At this stage it was a one-way telephone. The listener could only reply by telegraph, using Morse code. The first two-way telephone conversation took place in Boston in October. By now, Watson was working full time for Bell. They had made a transmitter that could also receive, so each could talk and then listen. The telephone became better and better, and the words more distinct.

Yet Bell did not forget his teaching. He hoped the telephone would soon earn him some money, partly because he and Mabel could then be married, and partly because he wanted to be free to follow his other interests. There was so much to be done for the deaf and so few people able to do it. He began organizing day schools for deaf children in several big cities.

Lecture audiences, such as this one in Salem near Boston, were amazed to hear disembodied voices talking from outside the hall by wire, through Bell's "miracle" invention.

28

Already news of the telephone was spreading. Bell gave many lectures and demonstrations, astounding eager audiences with his "miracle." No one had ever before heard a voice separated from a body. By his thirtieth birthday, Bell was becoming famous.

By 1878, the telephone had arrived in Britain. Callers spoke into the carved opening on the box and listened through the "candlestick" earpiece held close to the ear.

The lectures brought Bell some extra money and soon he felt wealthy enough to marry Mabel. They were married on July 11, 1877, and afterward they caught a steamer bound for England.

Bell showed his bride all his favorite places: Edinburgh, Elgin, Bath and London. In September, Mabel found that she was pregnant, so the return to America was delayed for nearly a year.

Bell and his telephone were already much talked about in Britain, and he was asked to give many lectures. He gave a private demonstration to Queen Victoria at her house on the Isle of Wight. The Queen described the device in her diary as "most extraordinary."

Soon, Bell and Watson were talking to each other while several miles apart. Important scientists often came to watch a new experiment, and sometimes newspaper reporters came too.

Queen Victoria had one of the first telephones in England installed at Windsor Castle.

Bell set up an English telephone company, which soon had customers in London and in the country, including Windsor Castle. But Bell was no businessman, and, at the same time, other inventors and scientists began saying that Bell had not invented the telephone and had stolen their ideas. Bell began to tire of the telephone and turned his attention to other scientific ideas. He was fascinated by birds, for instance, and sketched several designs for flying machines.

In May 1878, in their rented house in London, Mabel gave birth to their first child, a daughter. Five months later, after Bell had given a triumphant series of lectures on speech at Oxford University, the family set sail for North America – not for Boston, but for his parents' home in Canada. Bell wanted nothing more to do with the telephone.

6 ▼ After the Telephone

Bell's hopes of avoiding the telephone were soon dashed. As the steamer docked in Quebec, Tom Watson was there on the quayside, begging Bell to come to Boston. The Bell Telephone Company was in trouble and it needed him.

Bell, Watson, Hubbard and Sanders had formed the Bell Telephone Company in July 1877, just before Bell's wedding. When Aleck and Mabel left for England, several hundred telephones were in use in Boston and other cities. By the time they came back, the company was operating thousands. In the meantime, the huge Western Union Telegraph Company had begun operating telephone systems as well. It had been employing the brilliant Thomas Edison, who had much improved Bell's transmitter for them by using carbon. The Bell Company decided to sue Western Union for ignoring Bell's patents.

This was the first and most important of many such court cases. Bell's telephone patent was not only the most valuable ever issued but the most disputed too – over six hundred challenges were made altogether, mostly by impostors hoping to make a quick fortune. Not one of the challenges was successful. The Western Union fight took months, but with Bell in the witness stand, the company eventually gave up the battle and agreed to hand over all its telephone business to the Bell Company.

In 1880, Bell resigned from the Bell Telephone Company. Although he kept some shares in the company, which soon made him very wealthy, he had lost his enthusiasm for the telephone. Indeed, he later resented it a little because it could interrupt him so easily, and he always refused to have a telephone in his study.

Opposite The first page of a magazine article, describing the uses of Bell's marvelous invention.

TELEPHONE

Bell's telephone [1877]

GRAHAM BELL'S TELEPHONE

1876 has been a memorable year in the history of inventions. To commemorate the centenary of the foundation of the republic of the United States of North America, a World Exhibition was held at Philadelphia. As is customary at such exhibitions, instruments and machinery of various kinds could be admired there, bearing witness to the creative spirit of America's engineers and scientists and the imaginative flair of her most skilful tradesmen. Among all these inventions, there was one which not only contributed most to the fame of the Exhibition, but established the name of the United States as a nation of brilliant inventors. Yet it was merely a simple device which its

128

33

However, Bell did not stop inventing. He thought his next invention was the greatest of his life. He discovered a way of causing speech to make a beam of light "vibrate" in the same way that electricity vibrated in the telephone. Bell was so enthusiastic about the "photophone" that when one experiment took longer than expected, he completely forgot that Mabel was expecting their second child. When he reached home that February evening, Mabel was cradling their new daughter. In fact nothing ever came of the photophone.

Bell was very excited by his photophone, invented in 1881. In the transmitter, a shiny membrane in the mouthpiece made a beam of light vibrate with the pattern of speech.

The idea was simply far ahead of its time. Only now are optical fibers, carrying pulsing beams of laser light, slowly replacing electrical wires.

By now Bell was very famous and was receiving honors from universities and scientific societies the world over. Among them was the Volta Prize from France, which came with enough money for Bell to start a laboratory in Washington, D.C., where the family now lived.

The Volta Laboratory was a place where Bell and other inventors could work on their ideas. One of their first successes was with the phonograph. Just as

The receiver of the photophone turned the vibrating light beam into electricity, and then into sound. But the photophone worked only over a short distance, because light does not bend.

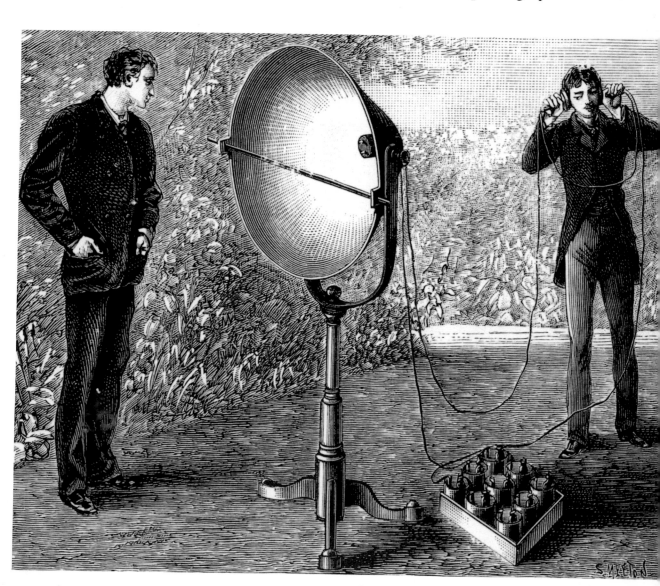

Opposite Bell and Charles Tainter called their improved phonograph the Graphophone. A stylus vibrating in the mouthpiece scratched the recording onto a wax-coated cardboard cylinder, rotated by a foot treadle.

Below Edison's original phonograph used a cylinder coated with metal foil, rotated by hand. The recording could be played only once or twice before it fell apart.

Edison's carbon transmitter had greatly improved Bell's telephone and so helped its success, now Bell improved Edison's phonograph. Where Edison had used dents in silver foil to record sound, Bell and his friends used a groove in a cylinder of hard wax and made the first practical record player.

Bell then turned to medicine. He made a probe that could detect bullets lying hidden in the human body and so enable doctors to remove them more easily. It was used for many years, until it was replaced by X-rays.

Another medical invention was his vacuum jacket, which fitted around a patient and used air pressure to help the patient to breathe artificially. It was a forerunner of the iron lung.

Bell never stopped his work for the deaf. He set up a school for the deaf in Washington and became the leader of a campaign to give every deaf child the chance to speak. Many normal people regarded the deaf as stupid or insane. They did not realize that children with normal hearing learn to speak by copying the noises their parents make, which deaf children, living in a silent world, cannot do. Alexander Graham Bell did more than anyone of his time to change the way people thought of the deaf.

In 1885, to escape from the unbearable heat of Washington's summer, Bell took his family to Cape Breton Island in Nova Scotia, Canada. Isolated, with bracken-covered hills, cool air, and salt water to swim in, it reminded Bell of his native Scotland. He and Mabel bought some land there and built a house with striking views from all sides. They spent every summer

Bell fell in love with the tranquil beauty of Cape Breton Island, Nova Scotia, in 1885. He spent his summers here for the rest of his life.

38

there for nearly forty years. Bell built a laboratory and farmed sheep on the hillside. He still worked late into the night and often, in the hours before dawn, he would run to the top of the hill behind the house.

By now Bell had changed from a tall, agile man with jet-black hair, into an imposing, bulky figure with flowing gray hair and a huge beard. His ideas never stopped. He made notes on the possibility of seeing by electricity (thirty years before television arrived); on measuring the brightness of fireflies; on putting a device in lifeboats for condensing drinking water from fog; and on a way of measuring the depth of water at sea using sound (which is how it is now done).

The imposing figure of Bell in 1904, relaxing with his grandchildren.

Bell had one more great ambition: to make a powered flying machine. Even after the Wright brothers flew the first airplane in 1903, he did not give up. In 1908, he and a few enthusiastic young friends won the trophy offered for making the first flight longer than a mile.

Then he turned his attention to boats – or rather hydrofoils, vessels with wings that skim the surface of the water. This was his last great project. By 1919, his hydrofoil reached a speed of over 68 mph (110 kph) – a water speed record that was held for ten years.

He had had one more encounter with the telephone. In 1915, the first transcontinental telephone line was opened, with Bell in New York and Watson in San

Above A powered airplane was first flown successfully by Orville and Wilbur Wright in Kitty Hawk, North Carolina, on December 17, 1903.

Left Bell spent many years designing hydrofoils – boats with wings below the hull. They "fly" through the water, lifting the hull above the surface. Bell achieved the world water-speed record with his hydrofoil.

Bell in his study at the Cape Breton house, toward the end of his life. He never allowed a telephone in the room – it might interrupt him!

Francisco, 3,000 miles away. When Bell said, "Mr. Watson, come here, I want you," Watson replied, "But it will take me a week to reach you now!"

Alexander Graham Bell did not do things the way others did them. He liked to work things out for himself. His independence, his individuality, which made him great, also made him chase the unachievable. Without this independent streak, he would not have wasted years on fruitless projects – but neither would he have invented the telephone.

On the first day of August 1922, at the age of seventy-five, Bell lay ill in the Cape Breton house. He was trying to dictate to his secretary. "Don't hurry," he was told. "I have to," answered Bell. He died the next morning, holding Mabel's hand.

His funeral took place a few days later, on the sort of gray, misty day he loved. He was buried at his favorite place, on top of the hill behind the house. Nobody wore black; the women wore white, the men their summer clothes. But, at the time of his burial, all telephones throughout the United States were silent out of respect for one minute.

7 Bell's Legacy: The Telephone Today

The name of Alexander Bell will always be linked to the telephone. Even though he left the Bell Telephone Company in 1880, the American telephone system was known as the Bell System for over a century. The company, which became American Telephone and Telegraph (AT&T), grew to be one of the richest in the world, operating over 100 million telephones and at one time employing over a million people.

It took much research to make the telephone work reliably over longer and longer distances. AT&T set up laboratories in New Jersey where scientists could investigate problems and make new discoveries. They are called the Bell Laboratories and now form one of the most important scientific research institutions in the world. Scientists working there have been awarded over 20,000 patents and have won seven Nobel Prizes.

In the early days, many regarded the telephone as a toy. This picture of party-goers exchanging New Year's greetings appeared in a London magazine in 1882.

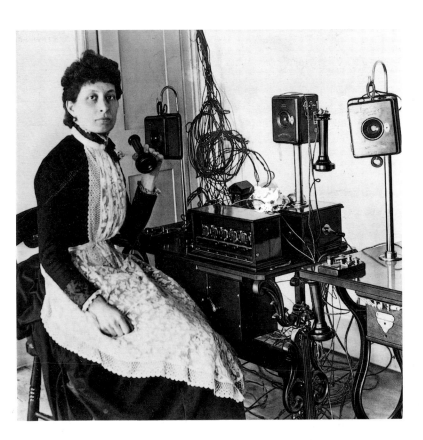

Bell's name is also remembered by the "decibel," the unit with which loudness of sound is measured.

At first, all telephone calls were connected by operators, who became an essential part of life (and often knew more gossip than anybody else!). Telephone dials first appeared in 1921, and now most telephone exchanges are automatic. The invention of radio early this century meant that people on ships, and those living in very remote places, could use the telephone. Now, even passengers on aircraft and trains can use telephones.

The last few years have seen a communications revolution. Satellites in space can receive telephone, radio and television signals from anywhere on the ground, strengthen them, and beam them back to another point on Earth. Telephones are no longer just for talking: computers communicate by telephone with other computers all over the world, and facsimile (fax) machines send and receive pictures, diagrams and letters by telephone.

Bell's idea of using light, rather than electricity, to transmit sound is only now becoming a reality. Beams of special laser light can be guided along flexible strands of glass, thinner than a human hair, called optical fibers. They can carry much more information than normal wires. By early 1990, there were over 25 million telephones in Britain alone, and half of all long-distance calls were carried by pulses of light.

We already have mobile telephones. Soon people will carry little personal telephones in their pockets, and fixed telephones in the home may become a thing of the past. Bell could not have dreamed of such things but his basic telephone principle has never changed.

Above *Colored light emerging from a bundle of optical fibers – the glass wires that are now used to carry light. Fiber-optics and lasers have made fast, high-quality communication possible.*

Right *Anyone with a mobile telephone can make calls from the street, a car or a restaurant table. Soon, it may even be possible to use a pocket telephone at the South Pole.*

Thanks to the imagination, inventiveness and persistence of Alexander Graham Bell, the world has become a smaller and less lonely place.

Bell's work with the deaf is not forgotten either. The Alexander Graham Bell Association for the Deaf, which he founded in Washington, serves as a worldwide center for information on deafness. His methods and ideas still flourish in schools for the deaf all over the world.

Bell's simple idea was so useful that our world could hardly carry on without it. He will be remembered as the person who helped to make the world a smaller place and, in more than one way, to bring the human family into closer touch.

Date Chart

1847   Alexander Bell born in Edinburgh.

1858   Aleck goes to school. Adopts the name Graham, becomes Alexander Graham Bell.

1862   Aleck leaves school, goes to London for year with grandfather.

1863   Begins teaching in Elgin.

1867   His younger brother Ted dies.

1870   His brother Melly dies. Aleck sails to Canada with his parents.

1871   Starts teaching the deaf in Boston.

1872   Opens his own school for the deaf. Starts experimenting with the multiple telegraph.

1873   Becomes Professor of Vocal Physiology at Boston University.

1874   July, sketches the first "harp" telephone. Hubbard and Sanders give him their backing.

1875   Patents the "autograph telegraph."
June 2, telephone receiver responds to "twanging." Bell becomes engaged to Mabel Hubbard.

1876   February 14, patent (No 174,465) filed for the telephone.
March 10, first words heard through the telephone.

June, telephone exhibited at Centenary Exhibition, Philadelphia.

1877   Marries Mabel Hubbard. Bell Telephone Company formed.

1878   Daughter, Elsie May, born in London. Bell Telephone Company starts proceedings against the Western Union Telegraph Company.

1880   Resigns from the Bell Telephone Company. Second daughter, Marian, born. Bell working on photophone.

1881   Bell and friends invent wax cylinder for Edison's phonograph at the Volta Laboratory.

1886   Buys summer residence on Cape Breton Island.

1908   Bell and friends win a prize for the first manned flight longer than one mile.

1915   First transcontinental telephone line opened, New York to San Francisco.

1919   Bell's hydrofoil breaks water speed record.

1922   August 2, Bell dies and is buried at Cape Breton Island.

Books to Read

Alexander Graham Bell by Kathy Pelta (Silver Burdett, 1989)

Communications by Ian Graham (Watts, 1989)

Communication Satellites by D. J. Herda (Watts, 1988)

Mr. Bell Invents the Telephone by Katherine B. Shippen (Random, 1963)

Sound by Terry Cash (Watts, 1989)

Glossary

Coil Many turns of insulated wire wound around a central core.

Conductor (electrical) Anything that allows electricity to pass along it, such as metal. A substance that does not conduct electricity, such as wood, is called an "insulator."

Current The flow of electricity through a wire.

Diaphragm A thin, circular membrane or sheet, held at the rim but free to vibrate in the middle.

Dissect A term used by biologists and doctors, meaning to cut open a body and examine the parts inside.

Electromagnet A coil, wound around an iron core, which acts like a magnet only when current is flowing through the coil, and stops being magnetic when the current is switched off.

Elocution Good, clear speech.

Iron lung A device used in hospitals to provide artificial respiration for patients whose respiratory muscles are paralyzed.

Laser A machine that produces a powerful, thin beam of light that does not spread out as an ordinary light beam does.

Morse code A code invented by Samuel Morse, in which letters, numbers and punctuation are represented by different combinations of dots and dashes.

Patent An official document awarded to inventors, giving them complete rights to their invention for a set number of years.

Phonograph An early kind of record player.

Physiology The study of how the body works.

Resistance A measure of how good a substance is at conducting electricity. If it is a very good conductor, it has very low resistance.

Resonance The way sound waves bounce around in an enclosed space.

Sound waves The vibrations of air particles that carry sound.

Tuning fork A two-pronged metal fork used by musicians. When struck, it rings at a precise pitch, depending on the length of the prongs.

Picture Acknowledgments

The author and publishers would like to thank the following for allowing their illustrations to be reproduced in this book: Mary Evans Picture Library front cover, 8, 10, 12, 34, 35, 40, 42; Eye Ubiquitous 11; PHOTRI 23, 27, 38, 39, 41; Ann Ronan 5, 18, 21, 33, 36; Wayland Picture Library *frontispiece*, 4, 1 6, 24, 26, 28, 29, 30, 31, 32, 37, 43, 45. Artwork on pages 6, 7, 13, 15, 17, 19, 22 is by Jenny Hughes. Cover artwork by Gill Andrae-Reid.

Index